New Vanguard • 8

Matilda Infantry Tank 1938–45

David Fletcher · Illustrated by Peter Sarson

First published in Great Britain in 1994 by Osprey Publishing,
Midland House, West Way, Botley, Oxford OX2 0PH, UK
44-02 23rd St, Suite 219, Long Island City, NY 11101, USA
E-mail: info@ospreypublishing.com

Transferred to digital print on demand 2009

First published 1994
7th impression 2006

Printed and bound by PrintOnDemand-Worldwide.com, Peterborough, UK

A CIP catalogue record for this book is available from the British Library

ISBN: 978 1 85532 457 2

Filmset in Great Britain

FOR A CATALOGUE OF ALL BOOKS PUBLISHED BY OSPREY
MILITARY AND AVIATION PLEASE CONTACT:

Osprey Direct, c/o Random House Distribution Center,
400 Hahn Road, Westminster, MD 21157
Email: uscustomerservice@ospreypublishing.com

Osprey Direct, The Book Service Ltd, Distribution Centre,
Colchester Road, Frating Green, Colchester, Essex, CO7 7DW
E-mail: customerservice@ospreypublishing.com

www.ospreypublishing.com

DEVELOPMENTAL HISTORY

In 1929 the Chief of the Imperial General Staff announced a broad review of establishments and organisation within the British Army, prompted by recent progress in mechanisation. He proposed to start with the infantry and two brigades were designated for experimental purposes, each supported by a light tank battalion, equipped for the time being with the tiny Carden-Loyd Mark VI Machine Gun Carriers, although such vehicles were entirely unsuited to the task. Exercises soon indicated that the infantry would expect their tanks to make the first break into enemy defensive positions, which implied a slow moving tank, well armoured to absorb heavy punishment.

By 1934 thoughts were turning towards a tank designed specifically for the purpose; an Infantry, or 'I' tank. The Inspector, Royal Tank Corps,

Major-General P.C.S. Hobart, detailed the alternatives; an inconspicuous tank, moderately well armoured and equipped with a machine gun, available in large numbers to swamp the enemy defences; or a larger type, mounting a cannon and armoured sufficiently to be proof against field artillery. The final decision rested with the Master-General of the Ordnance, General Sir Hugh Elles, the Tank Corps Commander in France during the First World War. Influenced by his own experience, Elles strongly favoured the concept of Infantry tanks and, constrained by a peacetime economy, he gave priority to the smaller type.

A11E1, the prototype of the Infantry Tank Mark I. Looking first at the suspension, notice how the return roller brackets share the same mounting as the main suspension units, the low setting of the drive sprocket and toothed front idler wheels. The front hull plate and the strong panels that support the idlers may also be seen while the open driver's hatch shows how it obstructs the gun. It also has no periscope mounting. (The Tank Museum, Bovington)

A11 Matilda

In October 1935 Sir John Carden, head of tank design for Vickers-Armstrongs Ltd., attended a meeting at the War Office with Colonel M. A. Studd, Assistant Director of Mechanisation. Sir John left with a draft proposal under the codename 'Matilda' for a small, two-man tank, armed with a single machine gun. Studd made two significant provisos. The design was to be ready within six months, and above all the new tank was to be cheap. It would bear the General Staff specification number A11.

Since the project could hardly be described as technically challenging the prototype, designated A11E1 (WD (War Department) No.T1724), was ready for testing by the Mechanisation Experimental Establishment (MEE) in September 1936. It was not an imposing machine. The low, narrow hull was surmounted by a tiny cast steel turret containing a single Vickers machine gun. The commander's head and shoulders almost filled the turret space, while the driver was located ahead of him in an equally cramped compartment with an overhead hatch which, when opened up, effectively blocked the turret and fouled the gun. The engine, a 70 hp Ford V8, was situated behind the turret under a sloping rear deck. It was linked

to a Fordson four-speed gearbox and Vickers light tank-type clutch-and-brake steering assembly driving the rear sprockets. The suspension, which was derived from the Dragon Medium Mark I artillery tractor, consisted of two stations per side each of which comprised four pairs of roller acting against quarter elliptical springs from central support that included a return roller. The tank also featured toothed idlers and medium pitch manganese steel tracks. Both these, and the suspension units, were totally exposed. Although the prototype was only constructed of mild steel it was built to a commendable 60mm standard at the front, and indeed relied on the rigidity of its thick plate for structural integrity, there being no internal frame to support the armour. The tank weighed close to 11 tons – about the same as a Vickers Medium, yet MEE always referred to it as a Heavy Infantry Tank – and had a top speed of around 8 mph, which was deemed sufficient to keep pace with infantry.

Early trials revealed the usual crop of faults, the worst of which was a constant failure of track pins. This was cured in April 1937 when the rear suspension unit on each side was lowered, which in effect raised the height of the drive sprocket by five inches. Similarly, since they wore badly, the

Another view of T3433 with the engine covers lifted. The Ford engine almost fills the space but ahead of it one can see the radiator and fan which separate the engine from the crew compartment. The catch on the left, and the cable leading to it, show how the covers are secured. They can only be released from inside the tank. (Vickers-Armstrongs)

two rear sets of rubber tyred road rollers on each side were replaced by all-steel ones. Complaints were also received about the driver's vision arrangements and turret hatch, but these matters were held over for improvement in the production machines, although in fact little was done until the second batch appeared.

The most significant difference between the prototype and production machines involved the turret, which lost its prominent lip and now featured a two segment hatch. These tanks had idlers without teeth and return rollers that were not linked directly to the suspension brackets while the tracks were located further away from the hull than on the prototype. Those from the first batch had headlamps mounted high on the hull, just ahead of the turret. The remaining 79 had them fitted lower down, near the nose, due to changes required when the mine plough was adopted, as explained later. Most A11s also had two stowage lockers, arranged pannier fashion either side of the nose.

Although there is no doubt that these little tanks were designed to be used against specific objectives in large numbers, for in practice they were little more than mechanised infantry machine

guns, they were never ordered in quantity. A contract for 60 was placed with Vickers-Armstrongs at the end of April 1938, and a repeat order for the same number just ten days later – about enough to equip two battalions. This was not due to excessive penny-pinching but a change in policy, and the final order to Vickers for the Infantry Tank Mark I, placed in January 1939, only amounted to 19 machines. The reason was that, with war now inevitable, it had been decided to produce a cannon-armed Infantry tank after all, and create up to six army tank battalions to operate them. The new tank was to be known as the Matilda Senior.

A12 Matilda

The first proposal for an enlarged Infantry tank dates from September 1936, although the emphasis at that time was on greater power and speed with a three-man crew rather than better protection, or even firepower. There followed three months of haggling over design priorities, which invariably stumbled over the problem of a suitable engine, and the search for a contractor, before the former was settled under GS Specification A12, and the latter in the form of

the Vulcan Foundry at Newton-le-Willows, Cheshire.

A requirement for two A12 tanks, at £30,000, was included in the 1937 Army Estimates. Although, in the early stages, an armament of two co-axial machine guns was proposed, this was quickly abandoned in favour of a 2 pounder anti-tank gun and co-axial Vickers machine gun in a three-man turret. In view of the tank's proposed role there were some who would have preferred to see it mounting a weapon capable of firing high explosive (HE) rounds. But the official argument was that these tanks were there to protect the infantry from enemy tanks, and at that time the 2 pounder was the best anti-tank gun in the world.

The problem of providing a suitably powerful engine was resolved by using two. The same solution had been adopted in the case of the Medium A Whippet tank of 1917, and once again the chosen power unit was from a London bus. But in this instance the selected engine was a diesel, an AEC straight six-cylinder water-cooled unit delivering a maximum 87 bhp at 2,000 rpm. Two of these engines were located side by side in the rear half of the tank, driving into an enclosed spur gear housing at the forward end of the engines which concentrated their power into a

single output shaft that passed down between them into a six-speed, Wilson epicyclic, pre selector gearbox, operated by compressed air from a Reavell two stage compressor. The output shaft from the gearbox passed through Rackham cam operated steering clutches into final reduction gears which connected with the rear drive sprockets. Cooling fans were mounted above the gearbox but driven independently by each engine's crankshaft, while the radiators, which could be swung upwards to give access, were directly above the fans. The use of twin engines was never a satisfactory compromise; it effectively doubled maintenance time and resulted in uneven wear to drive components unless both engines were perfectly balanced. The only saving grace being that if one engine failed the tank could just about limp along on the other, the redundant engine having been permanently declutched from within the fighting compartment.

The suspension adopted for A12 was known as the Japanese type. It was a highly interdependent system of bellcranks and horizontal coil springs first developed by Vickers-Armstrongs for the Medium C tank sold to Japan in 1928. It had been tested extensively on a British Medium loaned to the Vulcan Foundry during the design stage and proved very efficient where high speeds were not required. The tracks, at least on the prototypes, were of the single-piece stamping type with a deep H shaped indentation in each shoe, as developed for the Medium Mark III tank. The prototypes, and some early production tanks had track return rollers, but later examples used skid rails, which were much simpler to produce.

Despite earlier indifference it was armour protection that became one of the most significant factors in the A12 design. The hull front was an impressive 78mm and even the thinnest plates were 20mm, which was more than double that of a Vickers Medium. In fact the tank was capable of withstanding any known anti-tank gun and most other forms of artillery of its day. Structurally it was a mixture of rolled plates and castings with more than enough integral strength to offset the need for a frame. But since it was believed that the hull would take considerable punishment at top speed across country the upper and lower hull plates were rebated into the sides to reduce stress on the securing bolts.

Among the more interesting features was the nose, which contained the driver's compartment. Like A11 there was no provision for a front hull machine gun and gunner. On the instructions of the Assistant Director of Mechanisation this section was modelled on the imported Christie cruiser tank then being tested by MEE, yet the gaps that this shape would create between the nose and track frames were filled by triangular shaped tool lockers with top mounted, louvred lids. The complex shape of this nose piece was the main cause of bottlenecks in Matilda production. While the casting was suitably thick where it mattered it was also far too thick in areas where this was not important, creating an obvious weight penalty. It therefore proved necessary to grind away a good deal of this excess armour from the inside, a time consuming task which could only be undertaken with a great deal of care by suitably skilled craftsmen. The suspension, in marked contrast to A11, was totally enclosed, not only at the top but with deep side skirts containing mud chutes and complex hinged inspection panels.

The turret was a casting, with separately bolted top panels containing a drum shaped commander's cupola at the left, with a small loader's hatch alongside it. The loader was also the wireless operator for the No. 11 set (originally) housed in the back of the turret. The gunner was installed

The suspension adopted for Matilda consisted of two double, and one single, horizontally sprung bogies and the larger diameter, vertically sprung jockey wheel at the front. This diagram, from an early handbook, shows six return rollers (identified as track carrying wheels) which were later replaced by skid rails.

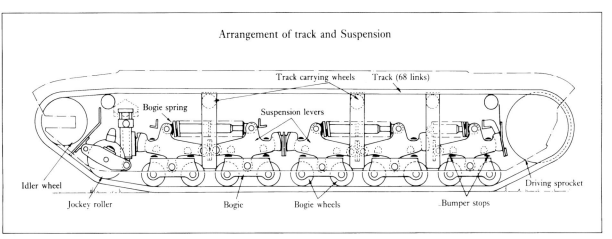

Arrangement of track and Suspension

Track carrying wheels   Track (68 links)

Bogie spring

Suspension levers

Idler wheel

Driving sprocket

Jockey roller   Bogie   Bogie wheels   Bumper stops

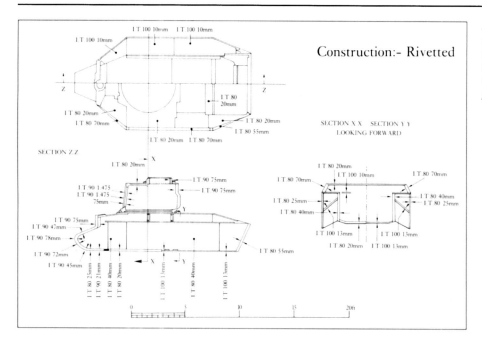

Construction:- Rivetted

SECTION X X   SECTION Y Y
LOOKING FORWARD

SECTION Z Z

ahead of the commander, serving the 2 pounder quick-firing (QF) gun and co-axial water cooled Vickers .303 machine gun. A pair of 4-inch smoke dischargers were mounted on the offside of the turret. Because the turret was a good deal heavier than anything which had gone before it was supplied with a hydraulic power-traverse system, but since firing on the move was now the accepted British method of tank warfare the gun was elevated and depressed by shoulder action of the gunner. This meant that the weapon had to be well balanced, which in turn required that a good deal of the breech end, behind the trunnions, was inside the turret.

From prototype to production

A12E1 (T3431) the first Matilda Senior prototype, arrived at MEE in April 1938. Following an initial 1,000 mile trial its performance was described as extremely satisfactory, apart from those cooling problems endemic to all new tanks. It managed a top speed of 15 mph, with plenty of power in hand and the only adverse comment concerned the tracks, which now had a bar tread added to each link that tore up the road surface. The way was now open for production to commence.

An initial order for 140 units was placed with the Vulcan Foundry in June 1938, followed in August by a contract for 40 from Ruston Hornsby Ltd. of Lincoln. Then, as the threat of war became stark reality, other firms were drawn into the programme; John Fowler & Co. of Leeds, the North British Locomotive Company of Glasgow, Harland & Wolff in Belfast and the London, Midland and Scottish Railway Company at their Horwich works. Vulcans remained as production parents to the group. Total production ran to about 2,890, including 20 completed in mild steel as training tanks. Unfortunately construction, even on this modest scale, was allowed to run on for far too long. Fowlers, who had experienced all kinds of delays and production problems, accepted what is believed to be the last order for 75 Matilda tanks in March 1942, which was not filled until some time in 1943 when such tanks were manifestly obsolete. In August 1940 when the British tank situation was at its most desperate, one Matilda was shipped to the United States for evaluation, with a view to having the type built over there. This was never done, but it had one most interesting side effect. Mr L. E. Carr, of the British Tank Mission in the USA, designed a power pack for it which featured a pair of General Motors two-stroke diesels, and this arrangement was later adopted for some American medium tanks, notably the M4A2 Sherman.

Matilda production line. From this angle the painfully small turret ring diameter is obvious. The turretless tanks still wait to have lids fitted to their hull toolboxes either side of the nose. At least two different patterns of track are visible. (The Tank Museum, Bovington)

1940 – failure in France

The War Establishment of an Army Tank Battalion in 1940 called for 50 Infantry tanks; three companies of 16 each and two with battalion headquarters. It also included seven light tanks for liaison and eight tracked carriers for transporting relief personnel. Clearly by this time it was hoped that all such battalions would have A12 Matildas (or possibly Valentines) because the establishment also showed a strength of 50 2-pounder guns. Reality was unable to match this. The two such battalions in France with the BEF in 1940, when

*Below: tanks **Dreadnought** and **Dolphin** receiving considerable attention from 4th RTR crewmen in a farmyard at Acq, before the battle of Arras. Both tanks have their turrets reversed so that the open hatches can be seen. Dreadnought's turret displays the Chinese Eye motif while on Dolphin one of its smoke dischargers is discernible. (The Tank Museum, Bovington)*

An early production Matilda Mark I, as yet unarmed, posed on a bank during trials. Concentrating on the turret one can see the commander's cupola and loader's hatches open, the sighting vane ahead of the cupola and the bracket for the wireless aerial which enables it to be folded down. (The Tank Museum, Bovington)

the Germans struck, only mustered 23 A12 Matildas out of 100 Infantry tanks, all of these with 7th Royal Tank Regiment. The rest, including all of 4th RTRs tanks, were A11s. They had clearly come to the wrong kind of war.

When the fighting in the West began the Germans simply did not oblige with the static defensive positions that Infantry tanks had been designed to assault. Rather they exploited mobility over a wide front and the Matildas wore themselves out trying to stem the flood. When they did make contact with the Germans near Arras on 21 May they proved invulnerable to German 37mm anti-tank guns. They were mostly knocked out by artillery fire, the exposed tracks of the A11s proving vulnerable. On the credit side these smaller Infantry tanks certainly had the edge on reliability over their bigger sisters. Some A11s, mainly section leaders' tanks, had been equipped with the bigger .5 Vickers machine guns, which could prove rather a handful for the commander. In addition they now had two 4-inch smoke dischargers on the turret and a No. 11 wireless set located up against the engine bulkhead below and behind the turret. In order to tune this the commander had to leave his seat in the turret and lie almost full length on the floor.

Apart from some engine trouble the wor failings of the A12 Matildas in France were th tracks. Once the indentations had packed wi mud they became virtually smooth and unable grip on soft ground or the pavé setts of Fren roads. Two modifications were noted on sor A12s. One resulted from trench-crossing tri held at Tilford near Aldershot in September 193 These had shown that a six foot trench, new made in soft sand, was too much for an A1 Being tail heavy it tended to drop its rear end in the trench and then found it impossible to cra out. The staff at MEE therefore devised a tail sk which fitted to the rear of the tank, between t tracks. It took the form of a steel box, flat on to but curved at the base, extending nearly three fe from the back of the tank. Further trials Farnborough proved that this worked on a six fo trench but was defeated by one seven foot wic There was talk of making an even larger skid, 3 9 ins. long, but no further reports can be trace The other modification concerned the suspensio There was some fear that the ground clearance A12 was too low, so the pitch of the suspensio was altered to lower the track bogies by s inches. This had the effect of raising the tank t the same amount, although it left the bogi exposed. It also placed excessive strain on tl suspension bellcranks which were now working an unnatural angle and more prone to breakin Like the tail skid this modification was seen c some tanks in France, but rarely afterwards.

Every single Infantry tank with 1st Army Tan Brigade was left in France when the Alli evacuated. All that remained in Britain was tl third regiment of the brigade, 8th RTR, whic was equipped with A11s and A12s on roughly two to one ratio. For some time this was the on complete tank regiment in the south of Englan available to resist an invasion.

Matilda Mark II

In the immediate aftermath of the disaster i France there was no time to make sobe evaluations. At least one senior officer did poi out that if the Germans were going to wage wa

ike this British tanks would soon be needing much bigger guns, but with invasion expected hourly the demand was for tanks of any kind to re-equip the army, so Matilda construction continued. It was still not very rapid. Before it could get into its stride the War Office was demanding changes in design, although these played havoc with production schedules. The first concerned the secondary armament. Just about the time when Matildas were entering production the War Office decided that it would standardise on a British version of the Czech ZB air-cooled machine gun, the .303 Besa, instead of the old water-cooled Vickers, in all of its armoured vehicles. This meant a modification to the Matilda turret design, not only where the co-axial gun passed through the mantlet, but also near the lip where an outlet, intended to discharge vapour from the water-cooled gun, was now eliminated. When the Vickers gun was removed the electrically driven pump that maintained its water supply went with it, and the circuit was modified

A Matilda Mark I from the first production batch built at Vulcan Foundry showing the suspension modified to improve ground clearance.

The strange device at the rear offside appears to have been designed to slice through barbed wire. (The Tank Museum, Bovington)

to provide for an extractor fan in the turret roof. In this form the tank became the Infantry Tank Mark IIA, or Matilda Mark II.

Matilda Mark III

No sooner had this matter been resolved than a search began for an alternative power unit. Both Fowlers and Perkins came forward with proposals but in the end a 7 litre Leyland diesel was selected which delivered 95 bhp. While the manufacturers worked at producing right and left handed versions of this engine the Vulcan Foundry set about modifying the second prototype, A12E2 (T3432) to receive them. This tank was also fitted, experimentally, with a complete Wilson gearbox and steering system, for which the designation Mark IIB was coined, to

Matildas Glanton *and* Gloucester *of 7th RTR, burnt out and abandoned a wood after the Arras battle.* Glanton *has one the louvres over its petrol tank opened to facilitate destruction. The louvred lids to the front stowage lockers caused an unfores problem. Items in them could be set alight under fire and the resulting hea and smoke prevented the crew from operating efficiently. (The Tank Museum, Bovington)*

signify a version of Matilda with the full Wilson transmission, although it was never used since the project was not pursued (the gearbox is preserved at the Tank Museum, Bovington). This tank also served as a test bed for the Freeborn automatic transmission system. Once the Leyland engines had been accepted contractors were ordered to fit them into future models, to be designated Infantry Tank Mark IIA*, or Matilda Mark III.

The Mark IIICS, IV, IVCS & V

During the early stages of Matilda development it had been agreed that the turret should be made capable of mounting a 3-inch howitzer, as an alternative to the 2-pounder, but this weapon was only required to fire smoke rounds as cover for the gun tanks so it could hardly be regarded as a major adjunct to the assault. The Leyland engined A12 was the first to be supplied in this form and was classified as Matilda Mark IIICS, for Close Support.

As the tanks saw increased service other problems were identified. One of the worst seems to have been the three point mounting for the engines, which were twisting in relation to their adjacent components, so the next modification to be introduced was a rigid engine mounting. The opportunity was also taken to improve the position of oil and air lines, and to increase fuel capacity.

Tanks produced to this specification we classified Mark IV or IVCS as appropriate. The is a homely little passage in the vehicle handbo which tells a crew member, who might want know whether his Matilda is a Mark III or Ma IV, to lift an air inlet louvre and peer at t nearest fuel tank; if it has an evacuation pun fitted then it is a Mark IV. The final improveme involved mounting a Westinghouse air ser directly on top of the transmission to impro gear changing, in place of the Clayton Dewand type built into the linkage on earlier models. Th seemingly modest change earned the designati Matilda Mark V; there was no Mark VCS.

Since, with the exception of the co-axi weapon on the Mark I, all Matildas look more less alike it is almost impossible to identify the accurately from the front. From the back tho with Leyland engines can be distinguished t exhaust pipes running down both sides of t engine deck; those equipped with AEC engin only display an exhaust pipe on the left side, sin the other emerges from the bottom of the hu although on all models the pipes ended in a pa of silencers mounted across the back of the hu beneath the overhanging rear deck. From t Mark III onwards the No.19 wireless set w fitted and from the Mark IV the turret signallir lamp eliminated, but the latter can only be seen

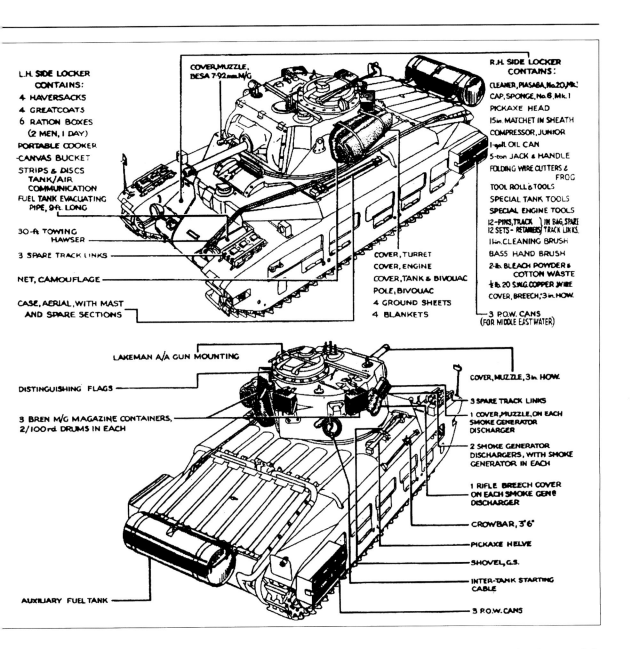

LAKEMAN A/A GUN MOUNTING

L.H. SIDE LOCKER
CONTAINS:
4 HAVERSACKS
4 GREATCOATS
6 RATION BOXES
(2 MEN, 1 DAY)
PORTABLE COOKER
-CANVAS BUCKET
STRIPS & DISCS
TANK/AIR
COMMUNICATION
FUEL TANK EVACUATING
PIPE, 9 ft. LONG

30-ft TOWING
HAWSER

3 SPARE TRACK LINKS

NET, CAMOUFLAGE

CASE, AERIAL, WITH MAST
AND SPARE SECTIONS

COVER, MUZZLE,
BESA 7·92 mm M/G

R.H. SIDE LOCKER
CONTAINS:
CLEANER, PIASABA, No.20, MK.
CAP, SPONGE, No. 8, Mk. 1
PICKAXE HEAD
15 in. MATCHET IN SHEATH
COMPRESSOR, JUNIOR
1-gal. OIL CAN
5-ton JACK & HANDLE
FOLDING WIRE CUTTERS &
FROG
TOOL ROLL & TOOLS
SPECIAL TANK TOOLS
SPECIAL ENGINE TOOLS
12-PINS, TRACK } IN BAG SPARE
12 SETS - RETAINERS TRACK LINKS.
1 in. CLEANING BRUSH
BASS HAND BRUSH
2-lb. BLEACH POWDER &
COTTON WASTE
⅓ lb. 20 S.W.G. COPPER WIRE
COVER, BREECH, 3 in. HOW.
3 P.O.W. CANS
(FOR MIDDLE EAST WATER)

COVER, TURRET
COVER, ENGINE
COVER, TANK & BIVOUAC
POLE, BIVOUAC
4 GROUND SHEETS
4 BLANKETS

LAKEMAN A/A GUN MOUNTING

DISTINGUISHING FLAGS

3 BREN M/G MAGAZINE CONTAINERS,
2/100 rd DRUMS IN EACH

COVER, MUZZLE, 3 in. HOW.

3 SPARE TRACK LINKS
1 COVER, MUZZLE, ON EACH
SMOKE GENERATOR
DISCHARGER
2 SMOKE GENERATOR
DISCHARGERS, WITH SMOKE
GENERATOR IN EACH

1 RIFLE BREECH COVER
ON EACH SMOKE GEN®
DISCHARGER

CROWBAR, 3'6"

PICKAXE HELVE

SHOVEL, G.S.

INTER-TANK STARTING
CABLE

3 P.O.W. CANS

AUXILIARY FUEL TANK

Stowage diagrams for a Matilda Mark IVCS tank. Notice the special Petrol, Oil, Water can racks fitted on each side to tanks in the Middle East, the auxiliary fuel tank and containers on the turret for Bren magazines when the machine gun is mounted for anti-aircraft defence. Oddly the artwork shows a low profile cupola but only one visible exhaust pipe.

it is elevated and the two aerials, which indicate the No.19 set are not always readily visible.

Tracks were changed, for a heavy box section, spudded type which was as useless in the desert as the smooth ones had been in France, but this could be applied to any mark. Later production models had more obvious external hinges on the suspension inspection panels, but this is no infallible guide, and the otherwise foolproof technique of relying on the WD number is rendered futile by the production changes. A contract card dated as early as 11 June 1938, for 140 machines, was subsequently annotated Matilda I, II & III without giving any indication as to how many of each were actually produced, let alone what their respective WD numbers were, and many of the subsequent cards are equally ambiguous.

A clear overhead view of a Matilda Mark I. On the turret notice again the sighting vane, close to the gunner's periscope and, on the other side of the turret the cast outlet for steam from the Vickers gun. On the rear of the hull the single top exhaust pipe shows up well while at the front notice that the driver hatch is closed while the visor in front of it is open. Alongside the visor is the driver's periscope. (The Tank Museum, Bovington)

Once the worst threat of invasion was over, and the tank supply situation somewhat relieved, opportunity was taken to give some of the older Matildas a thorough overhaul. The firm selected was MG Cars at Abingdon, Berkshire, and from one photograph taken there it seems highly probable that in many, if not all cases, new pairs of Leyland diesels were installed in place of the AECs. This makes identification of Marks extremely difficult and to a degree renders it almost pointless.

Later modifications

The size of the Matilda's turret was kept as small as possible in order to save weight. Coupled with the need to balance the gun, already explained, this meant that it was quite impossible to think of upgunning the tank, even though by 1942 this was highly desirable. The only alternative would be to fit a larger turret, and although there is photographic evidence to prove that this was done, no documents of any kind have been found to explain it. The tank is seen with a 6-pdr. turret of the type fitted to the A24/A27 series cruisers tanks, and an ugly combination it makes. But the turret ring on A27 was 57 inches in diameter, while that of A12 was only 54 inches. It would have been a drastic measure, though by no means impossible, to enlarge the Matilda's turret ring. It

is more likely that a larger ring was superimposed onto the hull. Photographic evidence seems support this. Yet the Churchill Mark III carried similar 6-pdr. turret on a 54-inch turret ring and this might have been a better solution. Following experience in France there was a somewhat irrational reaction against turret cupolas, and many late production Matildas, including most of those supplied to Australia, appeared with a low profile commander's hatch.

OPERATIONAL HISTORY

The spiritual home of the A12 Matilda, more by accident than design, was the Libyan Desert; indeed at one time it was known as the 'Queen of the Desert' and although this title has stuck it is not always easy to justify. Events in France have already been mentioned, and this theatre was the graveyard of the little A11. None of the 90 or so with the BEF came back to Britain. It seems that no one was particularly sorry to lose them. Even the few still in Britain were phased out of service as soon as something better was available. Yet there were nowhere near enough tanks left to resist the anticipated invasion, and in a desperate

The photograph that gives the game away. **Horace of 8th RTR in the MG works at Abingdon with an empty engine bay. The two AEC units, which presumably have been removed, stand on trestles. To the left a brand new Leyland set waits to go in, as does the transmission unit at bottom right.** *(The Tank Museum, Bovington)*

attempt to improve mobility some armoured regiments and army tank battalions (among them 4th RTR now re-equipped with A12 Matildas) were permanently attached to special trains, held in readiness at strategic junctions in eastern and southeast England, ready to be hurried to a threatened area should the need arise. This led to a series of trials in which Matildas and other tanks were seen climbing on and off railway wagons over all kinds of improvised ramps.

Largely for historical reasons the army tank brigades that operated Infantry tanks were formed from battalions of the Royal Tank Regiment. Perhaps they were not reckoned to suit the dashing image of the cavalry. But in an emergency dignity must take a back seat and at least two cavalry regiments, 16th/5th and 17th/21st Lancers both in 6th Armoured Division, numbered some Matildas among their Valentines while on home defence duties in 1940-41. In company with the four yeomanry regiments that formed 20th and 26th Armoured Brigades they normally ran two A12s with each squadron headquarters to provide close support fire and the advantage of three-man turrets. Even so they do not seem to have liked them, complaining of frequent breakdowns and weakness in the Rackham steering clutches after continual use on winding country roads. In North Africa it was a different story.

North Africa

The first Matilda battalion to arrive in Egypt was the indefatigable 7th RTR under Lt.Col. R. M. Jerram. After two months of acclimatisation the unit took part in various successful actions with 4th Indian Division which confronted the Italians, after their timid advance into Egypt, and threw them back on their nearest coastal stronghold of Bardia. It was during General Wavell's reconnaissance in force against Marshall Graziani's army, which began on 9 December 1940 under the tactical control of General O'Connor, that the Matildas earned their regal title. The 2-pdr. outclassed any Italian tank gun, the armour proved secure against virtually every Italian weapon and wear on the steering clutches became almost unknown. For one thing there was no need to turn the tank so often on desert terrain and for another the lateral motion of steering was far easier on Libyan sand than European mud.

Despite the early successes Bardia was considered to be a much tougher proposition. It was protected by an impressive anti-tank ditch and, during training with 6th Australian Division, 7th RTR created a replica of the ditch at Halfaya and developed means to tackle it. The simplest revived a First World War technique, the fascine. Unfortunately the Matilda was not designed to handle such a contraption in the normal way, by

The upgunned Matilda. A late production hull modified to accept an A24 style 6-pdr. gun turret, showing how the hull has been built up to take a larger diameter turret ring (The Tank Museum, Bovington)

launching it over the nose, so it was slung from the side. This required the tank first to turn itself broadside on to the ditch in order to drop the thing before lining up to cross it. A more sophisticated solution was a long, wedge-shaped ramp with runways spaced to coincide with the tank's tracks. It was supported on a pair of short tracked bogies and pushed ahead of the tank until it filled the ditch, whereupon the tank detached itself and drove across. Another local modification seen on one Matilda was a simple variation of the rolled carpet device, held on a pair of extended arms in front of the tank. It was unwound by the tracks while passing over barbed wire entanglements to form a path for wheeled vehicles and infantry. The regiment was reduced to just 22 tanks at this time, yet only one of these was permanently written off in the battle. When the assault on Tobruk was launched some three weeks later 7th RTR was down to about squadron strength, but the Matildas played their part well

although the majority were on their last legs.

Now, while the cruiser tanks of 7th Armoured Division headed west to inflict an overwhelming defeat on the Italian forces in North Africa, the surviving Matildas were carried east to RAOC workshops in Alexandria for a welcome refit. The kind of war that was developing in the desert was not one that suited slow Infantry tanks, and although the Matildas would continue to serve, when the front stabilised they simply did not have the mobility to cope with the rapid, fluid style of warfare practised by the Afrikakorps.

The role of the Matilda

Writing for his memoirs (edited by Sir Basil Liddell Hart as *The Rommel Papers*) after the

Battle of Sollum in the summer of 1941, Field Marshal Rommel noted that the British employed large numbers of Matildas which, on account of their thick armour, were impervious to most German anti-tank guns. He was, however, puzzled by their armament, explaining that the gun was too small and its range too short; he went on: 'They were only supplied with solid, armour-piercing shell. It would be interesting to know why the Mark II was called an Infantry tank when it had no HE ammunition with which to engage the opposing infantry. It was also... far too slow. In fact, its only real use was in a straight punch to smash a hole in a concentration of material'. Rommel was not alone in this opinion, General Wavell made similar comments and so, no doubt, did many of his tank crews, although their views generally went unrecorded.

The British view, as already explained, was that Infantry tanks should have an adequate anti-tank weapon with which to protect their infantry from enemy tanks, and in its day the 2-pdr. was unmatched. But it was not provided with a high explosive round, and even if one was available its explosive content would hardly have been worth considering. Thus, when confronted with some of the Italian frontier forts, the Matildas found they could make no impression upon them with their guns and had to enter via the closed door, like a battering ram. Likewise the Italian artillery, which always proved a tenacious opponent, could usually only be dealt with by very close action, and this increased the risk to the tank, for a large HE shell at point-blank range could be most destructive. Yet the real villain of the piece was undoubtedly

Huddersfield *of 8th RTR climbing onto a flat wagon over an improvised ramp of sleepers during trials at Aldershot station. The tank is finished in the early two-tone camouflage scheme and also exhibits the strange, blocked-in style of squadron markings seen on some Matildas of 1st Army Tank Brigade. (The Tank Museum, Bovington)*

took part in the 'Crusader' battles that resulted in the relief of Tobruk in December. By the following summer the conflict had moved westwards to the Gazala line, which was about as deep into the desert as the Matildas ever went but their numbers were much reduced. The renewed German offensive resulted in some very bitter fighting and by the time it was over, in June 1942 when Tobruk was retaken, hardly any Matildas remained fit for action. Four close support Matildas served with the Valentines of 23rd Armoured Brigade during the suicidal attack on Ruweisat Ridge at the end of July and the lone survivor could claim to be the last Matilda gun tank to see active service with the British Army during the Second World War.

the German anti-tank artillery. Used in conjunction with tanks in pursuance of Rommel's policy of concentrating firepower, it proved a very difficult target for a solid, 40mm round, fired from a moving tank. The German 50mm Pak 38 could penetrate the front of a Matilda using Composite Rigid shot and when they started using 88mm anti-aircraft guns against tanks it was clear that the Matilda had at last met its match.

Nevertheless the number of Matildas in the Middle East continued to grow. The 7th RTR, bolstered by the arrival of the 4th, took an important part in 'Operation Battleaxe' in June 1941, using tanks that had been rushed out to Egypt ostensibly for 1st Army Tank Brigade, the personnel of which was then at sea. Thus when that brigade was issued with tanks in September its senior regiment, 8th RTR, was provided with Valentines while 42nd and 44th RTR remained in Matildas. Elements of all these Matilda regiments

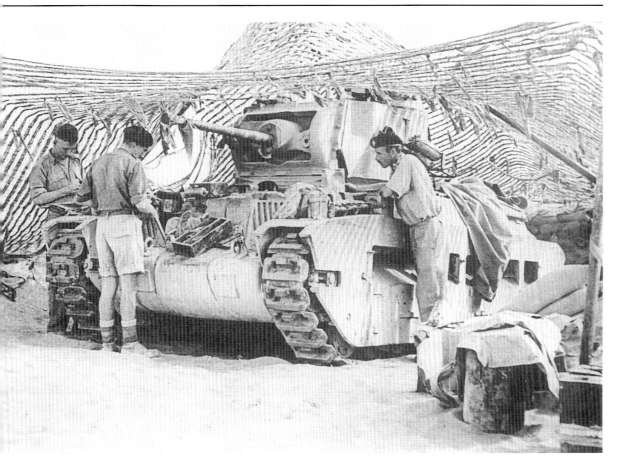

Eritrea

'B' Squadron, 4th RTR, equipped with 16 Matildas, was shipped direct from England to Port Sudan to spearhead the British attack against the Italians in Eritrea. Here, in terrain that was hardly suitable for tanks at all, this tiny force exercised a degree of influence out of all proportion to its size. In four months, during which nearly all the Matildas were maintained in running order by their squadron fitters and the LAD without recourse to any spare parts, since none were supplied, the tanks covered many hundreds of miles on their tracks and helped to defeat a much superior force.

The Mediterranean

Matildas were also turning up in other parts of the Mediterranean. Nine tanks from 7th RTR went to Crete in May 1941, only to be lost when German forces took the island. Matildas also joined the small tank detachment on Malta, where

A posed but effective picture of an RTR Matilda under camouflage nets in the desert with all four crew members at work. The louvred lids of the tool lockers can be seen in the open position and the tracks are of the original pattern with extra bars welded on. The purpose of the two square patches on the nose has never been adequately explained. (Crown Copyright, The Tank Museum, Bovington)

they adopted the distinctive camouflage scheme and made themselves generally useful without actually being called upon to fight.

THE CREW

The desert battles have been more than adequately described elsewhere, but the experiences of the men who crewed the tanks in action is another story. Loneliest of all was the driver, isolated in the nose of the tank. Either side of his seat he had the steering brake levers, which also acted as a parking brake, and between his

A poor but interesting picture of a 7th RTR Matilda carrying a large fascine during trials at Halfaya. Notice that to save weight, and presumably because ordinary timber is scarce i the desert, the fascine is a fabricated crib type. (The Tank Museum, Bovington,

the lever into position for the next gear he wou require and then activate it, as necessary, t dipping the clutch pedal. The clutch pedal w; replaced on the Matilda V by a foot-operate control pedal which peformed the same functio To the right of this pedal was the accelerato Compared with most contemporary vehicles th instrumentation available to a Matilda driver w; quite comprehensive. There were enough dial lights and switches to occupy three panels on th first three marks, reduced to two on the Marks I and V.

The driver's hatch was a curved, rolling hoo operated by a pair of levers, or screw device c

knees the gear selector lever. This acted in a single line, like the selector on an automatic car, and offered reverse, neutral, emergency low and five forward gears as it was moved away from the driver. The preselector system that was a feature of the Wilson gearbox allowed the driver to move

The Matilda pushing ditch-crossing ramps for the attack on Bardia. The bogie wheels and tracks are of the Universal Carrier type. (The Tank Museum, Bovington)

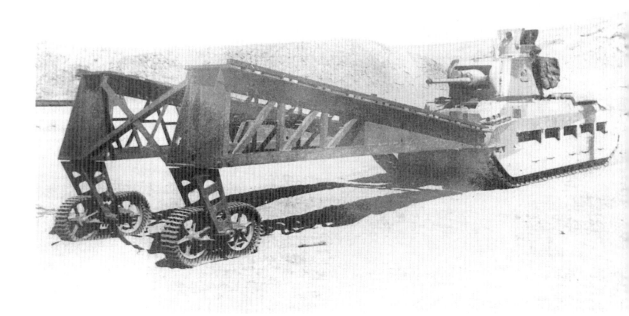

later Marks. When it was open he could raise his seat and drive head out. Closed down the seat was lowered and the driver observed either through a protected vision block directly to his front or a periscope just to the left of it. Although the hood was his normal exit the driver could also use an escape hatch beneath his seat but one suspects that this was a last resort. If his hood was jammed the driver was far more likely to try and escape through the fighting compartment. But to do this it was important to have the turret traversed right, otherwise he was trapped. Thus it was crucial that, upon evacuating the tank the gunner left the traverse control switch turned to the right so that, by starting the tank's engines, the driver could move the turret himself. Even so it was equally important, if the crew returned to the tank, to reset the switch before the engines were started, otherwise injury or damage could result. The starting up procedure involved declutching both engines by handwheels in the fighting compartment; for very cold conditions Matildas Mark IV and V were provided with ether carburettors which were charged from an Ethalet capsule through a device in the engine bulkhead.

Inside, the turret the commander's position was beneath the rotating cupola over to the left side. When the tank was closed down he occupied a small seat and observed through a protected vision device in the wall of the cupola, or a periscope set in one of the cupola flaps. In practice, particularly in the desert, these hatches were rarely closed, even in action; commanders chose the riskier course of working with their heads outside the turret, which improved the view, ventilation and chances of escape for the entire crew. In tanks equipped with the earlier No.11 wireless set, a switchboard gave the commander the choice of talking on the air or instructing his crew through their own headsets, although this communication worked in one direction only. When tanks were fitted with the No.19 set, two-way communication was possible with the crew and, over the air, the commander could converse with other tanks in the vicinity or, over longer distances, with his squadron or regimental HQ.

Ahead of him the gunner occupied a small, folding seat. In the firing position he leant forwards, his left hand gripping the handle of the power traverse or manual traversing gear as required and his right grasping the firing handle with his thumb hovering over the safety catch. The shoulder piece of the elevating gear was tucked firmly into his right shoulder and his

forehead pressed against the brow pad while he concentrated on the sighting telescope. This had 1.9 times magnification and was graduated separately for the main armament or machine gun, but with a narrow field of view. Thus it was normally the commander's duty to select the target and direct the gunner onto it by reference to a vane sight just in front of the cupola. This somewhat crude device was also employed when the tank was firing from a hull, or turret down

A wrecked Matilda photographed at Tobruk in December 1941. The hull front has been penetrated twice at its thickest point and again with even greater effect around the driver's visor. The offside tool locker has been torn open while the entire turret has been dislodged. Surely such damage could only be attributed to an 88mm gun. (The Tank Museum, Bovington)

position. The gunner also had a rotating Vickers tank periscope in the turret roof.

In action the loader balanced himself on the opposite side of the turret, using his right hand to steady himself and loading with his left, a 2-pdr. round being quite small and light enough to be held and loaded single handed. As soon as the gun was loaded he tapped the gunner on the arm and immediately took up another round. The semi-automatic action of the gun threw out the empty case and left the breech open ready for the next round. The loader was also responsible for firing the two smoke dischargers which were activated by bicycle brake levers and Bowden cables. There was a small, rectangular hatch in the turret roof above the loader's station, but his only other means of observing the outside world when closed down was through a protected vision device in the turret wall behind him.

A very uncommon sight. This Matilda has been fitted with a Sunshade device to disguise it as a lorry. A light framework has been created to resemble a cab at the front and the skirting plate has been painted to give the effect of a chassis and wheels. (The Tank Museum, Bovington)

FOREIGN SERVICE

Since it was in all respects a Vickers-Armstrongs design the little Infantry Tank Mark I was, theoretically, available for export sales under existing British rules. Such evidence as there is suggests that only one was ever sold, although the company records do not appear to confirm this. But it seems that in June 1939 a sample tank was purchased by the Polish Government and shipped out through Liverpool in August. Presumably it was intended for evaluation but in the event, to judge from a surviving photograph, it was used in action following the German invasion and duly knocked out, to the extent of having its turret dislodged.

Germany

German records claim that 97 of these tanks were captured in France, at least two of which were examined at the Kummersdorf testing ground. One, 4th RTR's *Derwent*, was pulled apart for a thorough examination but the type was considered underarmed and underpowered so if they were used at all by the Wehrmacht it could only have been on internal security duties.

The A12 Matilda would have been a much more valuable prize but the handful captured in France were not much use. Some, at least, were supplied to the High Seas Training Command based at Terneuzen on the Scheldt estuary. This unit converted at least one Matilda, nicknamed *Oswald*, into a self-propelled mount for a 50mm gun and, to add insult to injury, used others during trials for the proposed invasion of Britain. Some of those captured by the Afrika Korps were used against their former owners but, bearing in mind Rommel's comments, recorded earlier, they could hardly have been considered acceptable due to their poor mobility and in some cases their turrets were dismounted for use in fixed defences. Among those captured from the Red Army on the Eastern Front, some were converted by the Germans into extemporised artillery tractors by removing the turret.

The Soviet Union

Just over 1,000 Matildas were shipped to Russia, although some 250 were lost en route. Again their low speed and poor steering characteristics would

The driver's compartment i the Matilda tank tested in the US. The controls, whic are described in the text, include the steering levers, central speed selector and two foot pedals. All aroun are the switches and instruments on their variou panels while above one can see the driver's direct visio block, with the lever which controls its cover on the right and the periscope to the left. (The Tank Museum, Bovington)

have told against them where the battle raged over wide areas, but in winter conditions these problems were exacerbated by a tendency to clog up the suspension with snow or mud which became trapped behind the armoured skirting panels.

Canada

Commonwealth users of the Matilda, although not falling into the category of 'foreign' in the normal sense, still warrant independent coverage. First among them, but not often recognised, were the Canadians, whose 1st Army Tank Brigade was training on Matildas in Britain in the summer of 1941 before moving on to Churchills. This may have marked the start of their disillusion with British tanks which lasted until they adopted Shermans in 1943.

New Zealand

New Zealand also received 33 Matildas, all of the Mark IVCS type. They had been ordered in 1942 when plans were being prepared for the creation of a tank brigade. This was to be based primarily on Valentines but since there was no close support version of this tank the Matildas, which also had the advantage of three-man turrets, were to be issued on the basis of six per battalion. In the event they were never used. Priorities changed with the entry of Japan into the war and a year

later the brigade was broken up. One battalio was prepared for active service in the Pacific bu to avoid supply difficulties the variety of tanks ha to be kept to a minimum. For close support dutie 18 Valentines were adapted to mount the 3-inc howitzers from the Matildas and, since these wer now redundant, all 33 of them were handed ove to the Australians in 1944.

Australia

Often, when comparisons are made betweer British and German tanks of the Second Worl War, examples such as the PzKpfw IV are pointec to as having been in service before the war begar yet still remaining suitable for front line servic when it ended. It is claimed that no simila British example can be found. In the normal sens this is quite true. The PzKpfw IV had wha military designers call stretch potential, meaning that it could be adapted in various respects tc keep pace with developments and still hold its own. Yet the Matilda, which was at least designec before the war, could also be found fighting valiantly when the second great Axis surrender took place in August 1945, three months after VE Day had terminated the activities of the PzKpfw IVs. The reason in this case was not stretch potential, that was patently impossible; rather it was due to the Australian Army, which not only maintained and fought a temperamental, obsolete

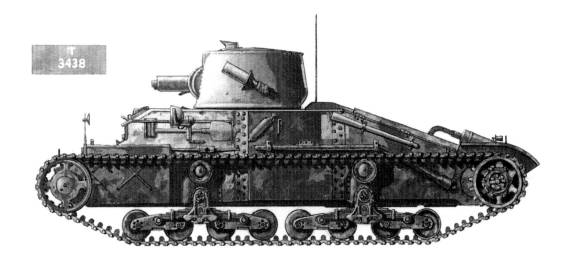

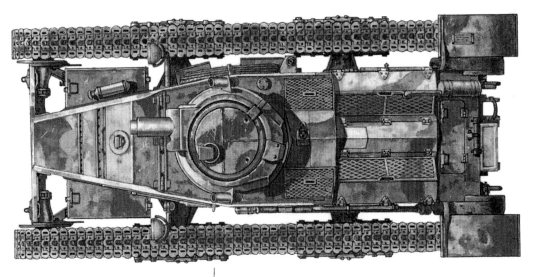

A11, Infantry tank Mark I
Derwent, 4th Bn.,RTR,
1st Army Tank Bde., BEF;
France, 1940

A

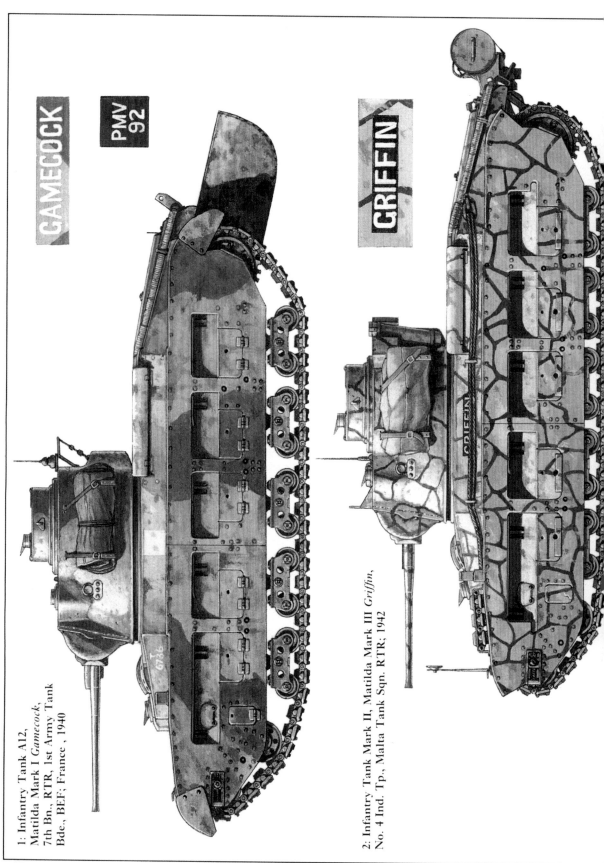

GAMECOCK

PMV 92

1: Infantry Tank A12,
Matilda Mark I *Gamecock*,
7th Bn., RTR, 1st Army Tank
Bde., BEF; France , 1940

GRIFFIN

2: Infantry Tank Mark II, Matilda Mark III *Griffin*,
No. 4 Ind. Tp., Malta Tank Sqn. RTR; 1942

B

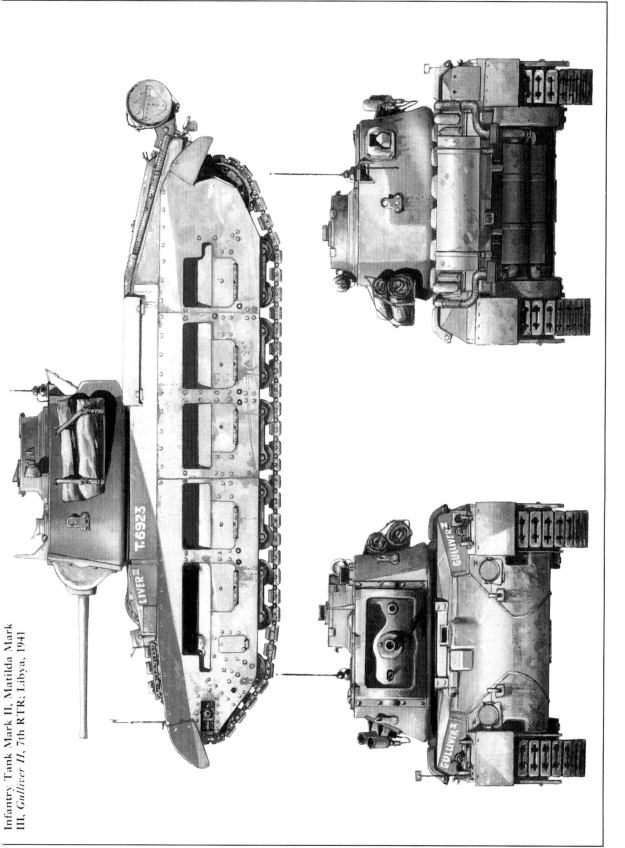

Infantry Tank Mark II, Matilda Mark III, *Gulliver II*, 7th RTR; Libya, 1941

C

MATILDA MK. III
7th Royal Tank Regiment, Western Desert, 1941

SPECIFICATIONS

Crew: Four
Combat weight: 26,924 kg
Power-to-weight ratio: 7.2 hp/ton (Imp.)
Overall length: 6.019 m
Width: 2.59 m
Height: 2.515 m (high cupola)
Engines: Two Leyland Type E148 & E149 straight six cylinder water cooled diesels, each 95 bhp at 2,000 rpm.
Transmission: Wilson six-speed pre-selector gearbox and Rackham steering clutches
Fuel capacity: 181.8 litres plus 163.6 litres in auxiliary tank
Max speed: 24 km/h.
Max. range: 80 km (on internal tanks).
Fuel consumption: 2.2 litres/km
Fording depth: 1m (with fording flaps closed)
Armament: Ordnance Quick-Firing 2-pdr. (40mm) Mark IX (52 cal), co-axial Besa 7.92mm air-cooled machine-gun
Ammunition: AP solid (1 kg)
Muzzle velocity: 853 m/sec.
Max.effective range: 1828.8 m.
Amunition stowage: 93 rounds
Gun depression/elevation: + 20°/-20°

KEY

1. Besa 7.92mm machine gun
2. Gunner's sight
3. OQF 2-pdr. Mark IX gun (40mm)
4. Gunner's shoulder piece
5. Commander's cupola
6. Cupola lid segment
7. Loader's hatch
8. Loader's seat
9. Commander's periscope
10. Lakeman anti-aircraft mounting
11. Bren gun drum magazine
12. Turret spotlight
13. Bren .303 in. machine gun
14. Aerial
15. Rear number plate
16. Spare Bren magazine bin
17. Right hand radiator
18. Auxiliary fuel tank
19. Left hand exhaust pipe
20. Left hand fuel tank
21. Three water cans
22. Left hand oil cooler
23. Mud chute
24. Signal flag stowage tube
25. Wireless set
26. Wireless valve box
27. Suspension spring
28. Commander's seat
29. Suspension bogie unit
30. Suspension lever
31. Compass binnacle
32. Gun recoil shield
33. Centre ammunition stowage rack
34. 2-pdr. ammunition bin
35. Suspension inspection flap
36. Gunner's seat
37. Sidelight
38. Turret traverse gearbox
39. Smoke cannister
40. Track tension adjuster
41. Driver's seat
42. Steering levers
43. Change speed lever
44. Throttle pedal
45. Towing/lifting ring
46. Headlamp
47. Driving mirror
48. Spare track stowage rack
49. Front stowage locker
50. Battery
51. Sidelight proctectors
52. Driver's hatch control
53. Driver's hatch
54. Shovel

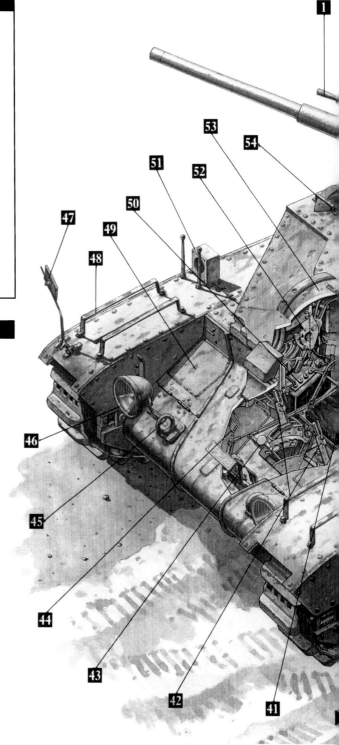

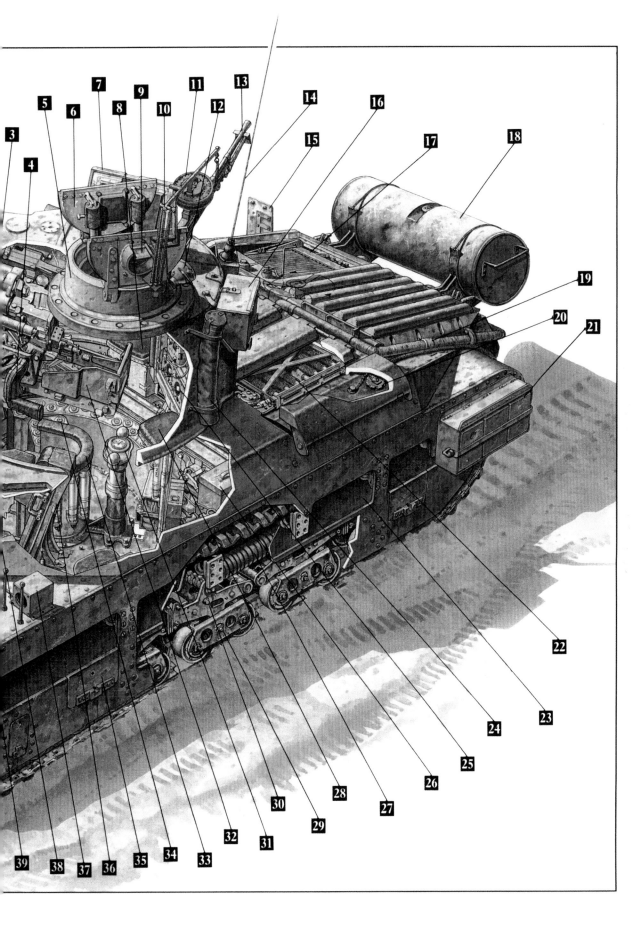

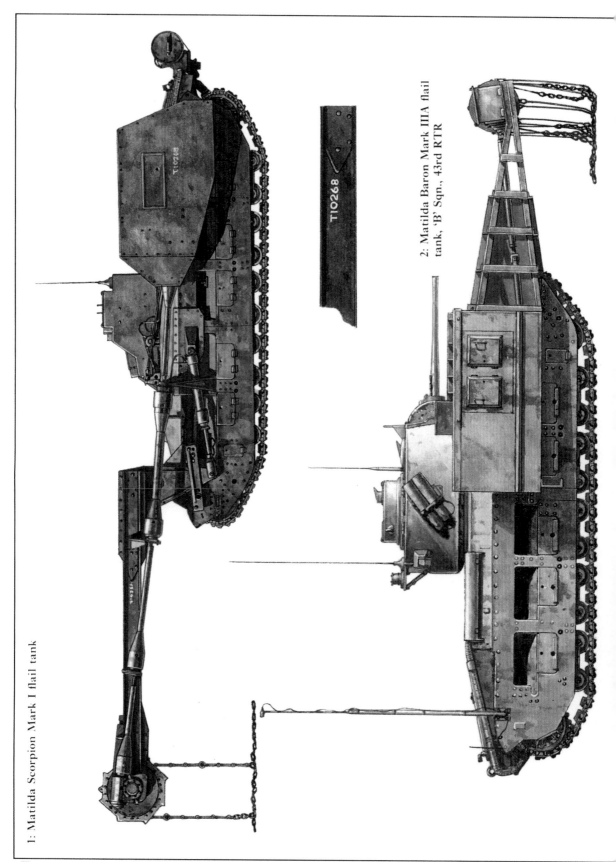

1: Matilda Scorpion Mark I flail tank

T10268

2: Matilda Baron Mark IIIA flail tank, 'B' Sqn., 43rd RTR

E

Matilda CDL and Matilda Crane tank, 49th RTR, 35th Tank Bde.

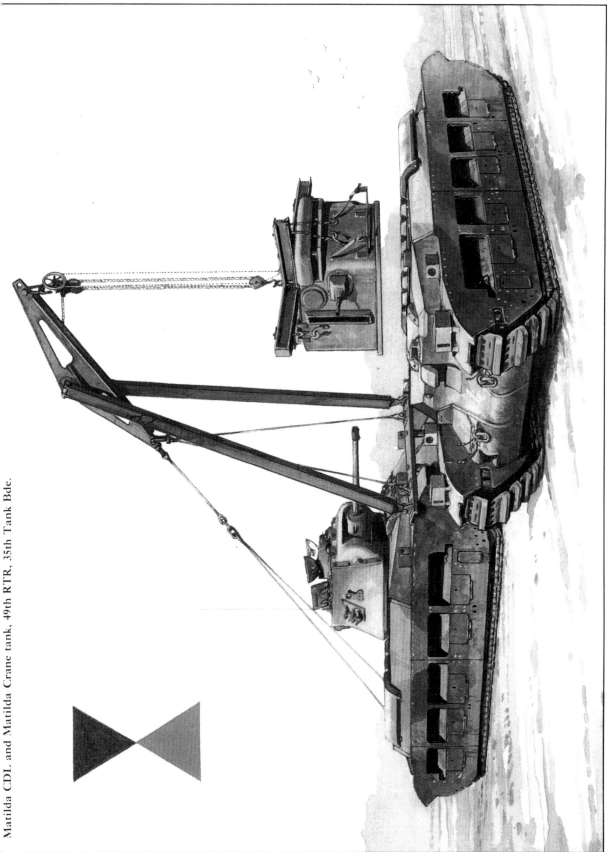

F

Experimental Matilda Hedghog rocket firing tank,
4th Australian Armoured Brigade; Queensland. 1945

G

ank long after it should have been retired, but also used it in a campaign where its greatest virtue, thick armour, was still a highly significant factor.

Australia is believed to have acquired 409 Matildas from Britain and New Zealand between 1942 and 1944 and there would appear to be no truth in the legend that they were worn out veterans of the desert campaign. Indeed all but a handful seem to have been late production vehicles with the low profile cupola and therefore, presumably, the Leyland engines, so there seems little doubt that they were supplied direct from Britain.

In addition to the specialised versions recorded later the Australians introduced a number of more general modifications. One was a semblance of turret ring protection, a feature sadly absent from most British tanks. On the Matilda narrow panels of armour were arranged around the front and sides of the turret ring. Some tanks delivered from Britain already had this feature in the form of bolted-on panels, but the Australians preferred to weld theirs in place. Another addition, probably designed to prevent tenacious undergrowth from

working its way in between the tracks and track guards in thick jungle, was a heavy cast shield fitted over each track at the front. On active service many crews took the traditional step of improving protection by hanging extra lengths of spare track around the front and sides of the hull, while expanded metal trackway panels were fitted at the back to prevent the Japanese from attaching sticky bombs or other adhesive demolition devices to the hull. In its final development this took the form of wire mesh panels on a steel frame covering the entire engine deck.

Although the Australian Government had raised a substantial armoured force in anticipation of contributing to the desert war this was rapidly slimmed down after 1943 when their primary commitment centred on the Pacific and what was believed to be very much an infantry war. Early experiences with M3 Stuarts did nothing to dispel this and it was only when the Matildas of 1st Army Tank Battalion landed at Milne Bay, New Guinea in August 1943 that the correct tank for this kind of warfare was discovered. Not that it was armoured warfare as any other Allied unit would have understood it, but it worked

Looking down into the cupola of the same tank, a Matilda Mark II, one can see the open hatches and the small pistons that support them, the periscope with the armoured lip that protects its head and the brow pad on the left which covers the vision block in the cupola wall. The handgrip control that moves the armoured shutter for this can also be seen, next to the knob that adjusts the spotlight. Laying on the commander's folding seat is his headset and microphone. (The Tank Museum, Bovington)

In German hands the Matilda was known as the Infanterie Panzer Mk II 748(e). This is the example nicknamed Oswald converted to mount the 50mm tank gun, seen here on a training exercise at Terneuzen. (The Tank Museum, Bovington)

admirably. The 4th Australian Armoured Brigade, which comprised 1st Army Tank Battalion (later 1st Armoured Regiment), 2/4th and 2/9th Armoured Regiments rarely operated at more than squadron strength. Beyond the assistance of the Armoured Squadron (Special Equipment) – which prefered to be known by its old title 2/1st Armoured Reconnaissance Squadron – with their Circus Equipment, the 4th ARB had none of the usual appurtenances of an armoured brigade. This was because it relied heavily for these on the infantry to which its squadrons were attached.

By VJ Day detached squadrons from the brigade were operating in various locations on New Guinea, on Bougainville, Tarakan and Labuan Islands and North Borneo. They were often fighting at troop level on roads that were no better than jungle tracks, bisected by fast flowing rivers and liable to degenerate into swamps without warning. The enemy remained largely unseen and the tanks were often subjected to point blank fire from artillery up to 150mm calibre which the Matildas mostly withstood, unless they were hit on their tracks. Probably for the first time since they entered service those Matildas equipped with the 3-in. close support howitzers now proved more popular than the 2-pdr. variety

since they could make an impression on Japanese bunkers.

Experience of these conditions led to further local modifications. First among these was improvised waterproofing which was essential for river crossings and the continual beach landings for in this campaign smaller types of landing craft proved more useful for tactical moves than tank transporters. The two exhaust silencers, situated across the rear of the hull between the tracks, also proved vulnerable and a shortage of exhaust pipe elbows to repair them resulted in experiments which transferred them onto the back of the hull each side of the engine decks. Finally an infantry telephone set was added to the rear of the hull which allowed the troops to communicate with the tank when it was closed down under fire. This reflects the increasing reliance that the Australian infantry began to place on their tanks once they had proved what they could do, even in the most incredible locations. At the same time it was soon discovered that the Japanese evinced considerable reluctance to face the tanks and often quit otherwise defensible positions once they heard the Matildas approaching.

Thus it was that these old war horses remained on active service right up to the end, even in the nuclear age. As if that was not surprising enough a few Matildas served with the Citizen Military Forces in Australia until about 1955.

VARIANTS

Towards the end of the First World War the British Army invested a lot of time and effort in the development of specialised armour; that is tanks adapted to undertake subsidiary roles on the battlefield, most of which were tasks normally carried out by the Royal Engineers. Between the wars this interest lapsed; nothing of any note was done until as late as 1937 and even then only in a modest way.

A German manned Matilda which has returned to British hands the hard way. The panel covering the transmission compartment is open and one of the radiators has been raised. (The Tank Museum, Bovington)

Mine clearing

As a first step consideration was given to means of defeating mines, which were regarded as a particular threat to tanks, and the agricultural engineers, John Fowler & Co., of Leeds, patented a coulter plough device which was designed to lift mines and turn them aside without setting them off. Following trials on a Mark IV Dragon the equipment was fitted to the prototype tank A11E1. It consisted of a girder frame, pivoted to the sides of the tank, which carried sets of blades and rollers ahead of each track. When it was not unearthing mines the contraption had to be raised clear of the ground, for which purpose a power take-off gearbox was mounted on the rear of the hull, directly above the transmission. Chains from the frame ran over pulleys on this attachment and, when raised, the plough was held above the driver's line of sight. Following trials, and all manner of modifications including the addition of wire cutters, the plough device was ordered for fitting to production versions of the Infantry Tank

Mark I. Production of the first 60 tanks then being under way it proved impossible to make the alterations essential to accept the plough, but they were incorporated into the design of the remaining 79. By the end of January 1940, 14 ploughs had been delivered, of which 12 were with the battalions in France, but trials revealed that the equipment would not work effectively in rough or frozen ground and it was never employed. In any case the opportunity never arose.

Plans to fit a similar device to the A12 Matilda were defeated by the complications of installing a power take-off on a more sophisticated gearbox so other options were considered. The Anti-Tank Mine Committee, which appears to have been both poacher and gamekeeper, was impressed by a French device that employed six large steel discs. Although deemed unsuitable as it stood a British version was created and fitted to a Matilda, but it proved too cumbersome for operational use. Rollers of a different sort had already been designed by Fowlers for British cruiser tanks and these were readily modified to suit Matilda, first

Matildas in Canadian Army service in Britain. Only turret squadron markings are carried and the censor has even obliterated the WD numbers. (The Tank Museum, Bovington)

with spoked rollers and ultimately as the Anti Mine Roller Attachment (AMRA) with a enclosed drum type.

The AMRA consisted of a frame, located o brackets attached to the tank's side plates, whic was supported on four broad rollers, arrange ahead of the tracks. Since a roller would b destroyed when it detonated a mine the syster had its limitations and could only be used t detect their presence. Once the minefield wa located it had to be cleared by hand, unless som other means could be found. One school o thought favoured sympathetic detonation, and th Obstacle Assault Centre carried out trials with device codenamed 'Carrot'. It came in three sizes the largest contained 600 lb of explosive, th second a 75 lb shaped charge and the third modest 25 lb. The two larger varieties wer carried on mine roller attachments which wer

automaticaly detached in the middle of a minefield, or against an obstacle, and detonated by remote control, hopefully taking all the mines out at the same time. Of 140 AMRAs supplied for Matilda 100 were earmarked for modernisation while the rest were put aside for Carrot trials. The smallest, Light Carrot, which a Matilda or Churchill could carry on its nose, was simply designed to be pressed up against an obstacle and detonated, without harming the tank.

The Matilda Scorpion

A far more effective method of destroying mines was the tank mounted flail. Again it had been considered before the war, but the system ultimately adopted derived from the work of the South African engineer Abraham du Toit. Having gained some recognition in the desert he was sent to Britain to develop his invention but unofficial experiments continued in Libya under Captain Norman Berry RAOC. Once the value of his work had been appreciated, in the late summer of 1942, some Matilda tanks were collected for conversion since by now they were virtually obsolete as

An Australian Matilda CS tank of 2/9th Armoured Regiment on Tarakan Island in May 1945. Spare track and panels of perforated trackway have been fitted to supplement protection and the rear decks are cluttered up with additional stowage. An officer, standing between the hoops of the jettison fuel tank mounting, is directing fire using the tank's telephone handset. (The Tank Museum, Bovington)

fighting tanks. Known as Matilda Scorpions they were modified at a Base Workshop in Egypt. Each Scorpion was fitted with lattice girder arms extending forwards on each side of the tank, with a rotating drum mounted between their outer ends from which hung the cable and chain flails. Power for the flail was provided by a Ford V8 engine, complete with its own drive train and cooling system, installed in a large box hanging from the right side of the tank. This box also housed the flail operator in supreme discomfort. Twenty four of these devices were available for the Battle of Alamein in October 1942, where they enjoyed some modest success, but there was plenty of room for improvement.

By the time the Eighth Army had reached

Tunisia, early in 1943, a Matilda Scorpion Mark II had evolved, in which the flail operator worked from inside the tank itself, but both models suffered badly from overheating of the flail engine. Mark II Scorpions were used during operations against the Mareth Line defences but by now the Matilda was being regarded as too slow for the work; not that the actual flailing could be done any faster but because there were not enough of them to do all the mine clearing required, and they were not fast enough to move quickly from one job to another.

The Matilda Baron

Meanwhile in Britain, du Toit, working in conjunction with AEC Ltd., continued to develop his ideas. Again the Matilda served as the basis but the codename selected here was 'Baron'. The prototype, designated Mark I, which used a Chrysler engine with chain and sprocket drive to the flail, was redeveloped as the Mark II which employed a Bedford engine and shaft drive. I both forms this prototype retained its 2-pdr. turr and had the flail engine housed on the right sid The production version was a major developmen The turret was replaced by a fixed superstructu and two Bedford engines were used, slung on eac side of the tank. The object was to supply mo power since it had now been decided to exten the scope of the Baron so that, in addition t flailing, it could chop its way through barbed wi and even excavate earthworks by lowering i rotor, which was formed from cross girders rath than a drum. This version appeared first as th Matilda Baron Mark III and, in slightly improve form, as the Mark IIIA, 60 of which were built b

An Australian Matilda in post-war service with the Citizen Military Force, having a track fitted. One of the armoured shields which protects the idler has been swung back and, presumably to avoid damage, the side racks hav been moved to a position o top of the track guards. (P. Handel)

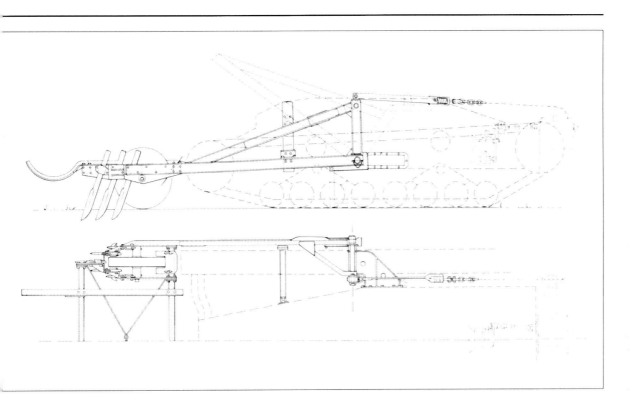

Curran Brothers of Cardiff and issued for training and demonstrations, although they never saw active service.

The Canal Defence Light (CDL)

The history of the device known as the Canal Defence Light (CDL) is too involved to be included here but it is important for its associations with the Matilda tank. Indeed it was the Matilda that was first selected for conversion to this role and which, at one time, equipped four out of the five Royal Armoured Corps regiments trained to operate it. To convert the tank, the original turret was replaced by a special pattern built to a 65mm armour standard, which contained a carbon arc lamp that projected an eight million candle-power beam. Using mirrors the beam was directed through a vertical slit in the turret front, protected by a moving shutter which reduced the risk from small-arms fire and caused the light to flicker. Half of the turret, on the left, was partitioned off and occupied by the operator who controlled the light, replaced burnt out carbons and used the tank's only armament, a Besa machine gun, if required. The driver, the

Drawings taken from the original patent documents show the Fowler Coulter Plough minesweeping device as fitted to A11E1. In addition to the tines and rollers one can see the lifting apparatus at the back and the gearbox take-off that operated it. The broken lines show where it was held in the lifted position.

only other crew member, doubled as the wireless operator.

The entire CDL project was regarded as highly secret and in Britain trials were conducted in a secluded part of the Lake District. As an adjunct to night attacks the CDL tanks would line up, about 100 yards apart, and cause their beams to intercept some 300 yards from the base line, creating triangles of darkness in which attacking troops could operate. Defenders would be dazzled and, firing blind, could only inflict casualties by chance, whereas the attackers had a clear view of their objectives. Two Army Tank Brigades (1st and 35th) were converted to this role between 1941 and 1944 and from the latter 42nd Royal Tank Regiment was despatched to Egypt as the basis for a brigade to be formed out there. A CDL regiment was planned on the basis of 42

The Fowler Coulter Plough device fitted to A11EI. The equipment is in the raised, or travelling position and it is also fitted with the tubular steel wire cutters.

searchlight tanks and 19 gun tanks, the latter to serve as troop and squadron leader's tanks plus four, probably of the close support type, with regimental headquarters. A system was therefore devised by which gun tanks could be converted instantly to the CDL role and vice versa. The scheme involved a 5-ton capacity crane attachment that could be mounted on any Matilda enabling it to swap over turrets as required. The only other task then being to fit an extra generator, belt driven from a pulley on the drive shaft. Matilda CDL tanks were also fitted with a low visibility, monoslot headlamp on each track guard, almost a CDL in miniature, for ordinary night driving.

As a subject for CDL conversion a Matilda had the advantages of being available in quantity, well armoured and reasonably reliable. Against this it

was slow, had to run its main engines in order drive the generator when the light was being us and, with only a two-man crew, was a bit of handful to operate. By 1943 it was also rath outdated and was duly replaced in the survivir CDL regiments by M3 Lee and Grant tanks.

Other variants

Apart from those minor modifications covered the previous section there were one or tw experimental versions of Matilda developed Britain which deserve a mention. 'Black Prince' w the codename given to a radio-controlled prototy which appeared in 1941. It was based on A12E with the full Wilson transmission which could l activated by remote control. The experiment had variety of aims. One was to create a mobile targ tank, which was abandoned on the grounds extravagance. Another was to use the tank as means of drawing enemy fire to reveal locations hidden anti-tank guns and it was also considered a crewless tank for sacrificial, demolition missions. An order for 60 was cancelled once it was realised that all the tanks would have to have their transmissions modified since the Rackham clutches were not suitable for remote activation. Another Matilda was adapted to carry a single length of Bangalore torpedo, in crutches, on the nearside skirting plate. This could be elevated when required and then fired into barbed wire entanglements to cut a path for infantry. A project that harked back to the First World War had a Matilda pushing a long section of Inglis portable bridge, on dumb caterpillar tracks, which it could propel across a gap under fire and then drive over into action.

Australian variants

The Australian Army developed its own range of modified Matildas under the collective title of Circus Equipment, designed in response to the requirements of jungle warfare.

The original Fowler roller device attached to a Matilda in Egypt. The rollers are of the open, spoked pattern with what appear to be studs on the outer surface. (The Tank Museum, Bovington)

Tank bulldozers

The first of these was a tank bulldozer, using a Britstand full-width blade manufactured by the British Standard Machinery Co., of Sydney. It came in two forms; the No.1 Mark I used cables to raise and lower the blade while the No.3 Mark I used hydraulics, activated by a Hydreco oil pump driven by chain and sprocket from the propellor shaft. The former type was used by 2/1 Australian Armoured Brigade Reconnaissance Squadron during the landings on Labuan and Balikapan in August 1945, but with no apparent success. The extra weight of the blade and pushpoles kept the nose of the tank down, causing the blade to dig in. The tank driver was unable to see what he was doing while bulldozing and, even with the Rackham clutches in perfect condition, it was very difficult to steer. The second version was supplied as a field fitting kit at the end of the war, but even this caused problems due to poor manufacturing standards. Most of the shortcomings already encountered with the first model were repeated in the second. The original idea had been to use the dozer tanks to remove obstacles under fire, fill in craters in roads or, as a

last resort, bury occupied Japanese bunkers, while the tanks were capable of jettisoning their blades and acting as conventional tanks if necessary.

The Frog

The Australian flamethrower version of Matilda was known as the 'Frog'. The projector was mounted in place of the main armament, within a tube designed to resemble the 3-inch howitzer, and the co-axial Besa machine gun was retained. In order to avoid the complication of feeding flame fuel through a rotary junction at the turret base the main fuel and compressed air propellant tanks were located within the turret. This left it cramped for the remaining crew member after the redundant gunner and loader had been omitted. Eighty gallons of a thickened flame fuel called Geletrol were stored in this internal tank with a further 100 gallons in an external jettison tank at the back, 30 gallons in tanks which replaced the tool lockers on either side of the nose and another 32 gallons shared between four small tanks in the sides of the hull. It was hardly an ideal arrangement and the system for replenishing the main tank from the reserves was complicated but essential. The Frog fired out to a range of about 90 yards and used ten gallons in every burst. When they were used on Borneo the flamethrowers proved very effective against Japanese positions, although it was considered a nuisance that, with the existing pressure feed system, there was a 30 second pause between bursts for the pressure to build up again. Not surprisingly it seems that the front and side reserve tanks were never filled when the Frog went into action, and even the jettison tank could prove vulnerable in thick jungle conditions. An improved Matilda flamethrower codenamed 'Murray' employed cordite as a propellant. This not only speeded up the rate of fire but allowed more space in the turret, which now had an increased flame fuel capacity of 130 gallons although this appeared too late to be used in action during the war.

The Projector

The last Australian Matilda conversion was certainly the most ambitious, and probably the most spectacular in effect although it was never employed operationally. This was the 'Projector' Hedgehog No.1 Mark I. It stemmed from an original scheme to launch an anti-submarine depth charge from a tank against enemy bunkers, but was modified to fire a battery of smaller projectiles. The conversion involved fitting a seven chambered launcher box to the back of the tank, above the engine louvres. It was pivoted at the rear and raised or lowered by hydraulics adapted from the Logan turret traverse apparatus from an American M3 Medium tank. In the

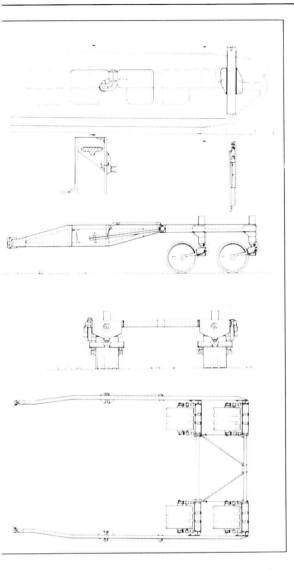

*diagram from the Anti-
ine Roller Attachment
indbook showing the
uipment and the brackets
hich attach it to the tank.*

*The assembly pivots on the
rear bearing and is free to
slide within the front
bracket.*

avelling position the launcher, which was
rotected by an armoured shield, lay flat within a
w, three-sided superstructure. To fire it was
evated to 45 degrees and aimed by pointing the
nk.

The projectiles, which were also naval anti-
ibmarine weapons, each weighed 63 lbs but were
1odified to accept a percussion fuse. Range was
etween 200-300 yards, depending on the
ropellant used, and firing was initiated

electrically. Bombs 1, 2, 3, 4, 6 and 7 were fired
with the turret at 12 o'clock but it had to be
traversed to 1 o'clock when round No. 5 was fired
to spare the wireless aerial. Results of trials
carried out at Southport, Queensland, in May
1945 suggest that as a bunker busting weapon the
Hedgehog would have been impressive. Accuracy
was stated to be adequate for all practical
purposes and the commander of 4th Australian
Brigade commented: 'The conduct of the trial left
nothing to be desired and was carried out to my
entire satisfaction'.

THE PLATES

Plate A: *A11, Infantry Tank Mark I Derwent,
4th Battalion, Royal Tank Regiment, 1st Army
Tank Brigade, BEF; France, 1940*
In accordance with War Office instructions this
tank is painted in khaki green with a disruptive
pattern of dark green. Twelve inch square white
markings on all surfaces were adopted as the
British recognition sign and the palette shaped
patch of greenish-yellow colour in front of the
driver's visor is a gas-sensitive paint which changes
hue in the presence of poison gas.

The white figure '4' on a red square was the
unit identification while the white bar across the
top indicates that the brigade was operating as
corps troops; in this case 1st Corps. Since the
figure was the same for both battalions they can
best be distinguished by the vehicle's name, the
initial letter of which matched its order in the
alphabet. The 4th Battalion, however, also used
the traditional Chinese Eye inherited from 6th
Battalion, Tank Corps in 1919. Other markings on
this tank are the War Department (WD) number,
T3438, and the civil registration plate HMH793
drawn, as were most pre-war British military
vehicles, on groups issued to Middlesex County
Council.

Derwent was from the first batch of A11s to be
built. It was the tank selected by the Germans for
complete evaluation, which resulted in its
destruction.

Plate B1: *Infantry Tank A12, Matilda Mark I Gamecock, 7th Battalion, Royal Tank Regiment, 1st Army Tank Brigade, BEF; France 1940*

This tank also sports the khaki green and dark green disruptive camouflage scheme and the white identification squares peculiar to the BEF, however the Matildas of 7th RTR seem rarely to have carried unit identification plates, if at all. Thus the only other markings are the WD and registration numbers plus the name, painted somewhat unusually across the back. This tank was photographed after capture and is thus known to be one which had the modified suspension and trench-crossing tail skid attachment.

Plate B2: *Infantry Tank Mark II, Matilda Mark III, Griffin, No. 4 Independent Troop, Malta Tank Squadron, Royal Tank Regiment; 1942*

The tank detachment on Malta adopted a curious camouflage scheme dictated by local conditions. Much of the island being exposed and bare the most common feature was the stone walling that lined the roads and surrounded the fields, so the vehicles were painted to blend in with this. Other markings were entirely absent except for individual tank names which they seem to have retained from their previous service. Thus *Griffin*, and possibly its crew, was ex-7th RTR. At least three Matildas are known to have served on Malta.

A variety of tanks passed through the hands the Independent Troop including Light Mark V A9 and A13 Cruisers and some Valentines.

Plate C: *Infantry Tank Mark II, Matilda Mar III, Gulliver II, 7th Royal Tank Regimen Libya, 1941*

Gulliver II of 7th RTR exhibits one of the mo interesting, and controversial camouflage schem ever applied to British tanks. Based on naval ide originally adopted in the First World War i purpose was to disguise the outline of the tan and thus deceive enemy gunners, rather tha

A Matilda Scorpion II flail tank showing the modified girder arrangement. Viewed from this side one can see the Crusader type air-filter inboard of the engine housing and the wedge-shaped fitting at the back. In this version the flail operator formed part of th turret crew.

The original Matilda Baron flail, probably in its second guise, showing the open style rotor in the raised position and the complicated system of linked chains adopted for the Baron. (The Tank Museum, Bovington)

end it into the background. Two shades of grey, probably drawn from Royal Navy stores, are applied over the base light sand colour. There was nothing random about the design, it was worked out with mathematical accuracy and, as may be seen by half closing the eyes, had a remarkable ability to apparently alter the shape of the tank. This effect was later spoiled to some extent by the application of large white/red/white identification panels painted on the hull and turret sides of many tanks.

As in France 7th RTR seem to have been averse to using any other markings on their Matildas beyond the obligatory WD number and individual tank name.

Plate D: *Infantry Tank Mark IIA*, Matilda Mark III*

Original specifications, issued in 1939, described an authorised shade of aluminium (silver) paint for all interior surfaces on British tanks but then qualified this by explaining that any similar shade was acceptable and, indeed, any other suitable colour if no silver paint was obtainable. It would seem that there was no authorised colour for mechanical components and these were fitted as supplied by the manufacturer, usually in natural metal finish. That portion of the gun tube inside the turret was finished in the external colour, with natural metal breech block, but it may not have been repainted in sand before the first major overhaul. Ready-use ammunition was stowed in

and around the turret basket with the reserve stock easily accessible in the adjacent hull sponsons. However it should be noted that no ammunition was stowed above turret ring level. The standard anti-tank round was a solid steel projectile with tracer in the base, painted black with a white and red banded nose cap. The earlier armour piercing shell proved faulty and was discontinued, while tanks never carried the pathetic high-explosive shell. An armour piercing capped, ballistic capped (APCBC) appeared too late for Matildas serving in the desert.

Plate E1: *Matilda Scorpion Mark I flail tank*

Elements of 6th, 42nd and 44th Royal Tank Regiments operated Matilda Scorpion flail tanks at second Alamein, albeit with limited success. Most crews appear to have discarded the access panel on the side of the auxiliary engine housing, presumably in an effort to reduce the operating temperature of the Ford V8. The drive shaft, connecting this engine with the flail rotor, can be seen passing through the boom girders. Viewed from this side of the tank the flails would be turning in a clockwise direction. Also visible are the tall station-keeping indicators at the back, which were often all that could be seen of the tank in action. None of these tanks appear to have been camouflage painted at this stage and the only marking visible is the WD number, in black, on the side of the flail motor box and across the rear of the hull.

The Matilda modified to demonstrate the flying Bangalore torpedo equipment. The explosive tube rests in crutches on t[...] side. To fire it is elevated from the bracket at the back and launched by remote control from withi[...] the tank. The spiked colla[...] near the leading end cause[...] it to catch in a barbed wi[...] entanglement before detonating. (The Tank Museum, Bovington)

Plate E2: *Matilda Baron Mark IIIA flail tank, 'B' Squadron, 43rd Royal Tank Regiment*
Matilda Barons used for training in Britain were finished in the khaki brown shade from late 1942 until 1944. Again there is no evidence of unit or squadron markings being applied although the WD number, in white, was painted on the flail motor housings, repeated on the flail boom girders, on the back of the hull and across the front of the crew compartment.

Three features worth noting are the hydraulic cylinder, multi-jointed flail rotor drive shaft ar[...] the flail motor exhaust and silencer emerging fro[...] beneath the housing. Viewed from this side t[...] flails would rotate in an anti-clockwise direction.

Plate F: *Matilda Canal Defence Light a[...] Matilda Crane tank, 49th Royal Tan[...] Regiment, 35th Tank Brigade*
In this picture a Matilda fitted with a portab[...] crane attachment is in the process of converting [...] 2-pdr. gun tank into a CDL. The crane has lift[...]

The Matilda Restive being used to demonstrate the launching procedure for an Inglis bridge on tracks. The main alteration to the tank involved fitting a massive bracket to the nose. Notice how the rear number plate has been repainted to show the WD number. (The Tank Museum, Bovington)

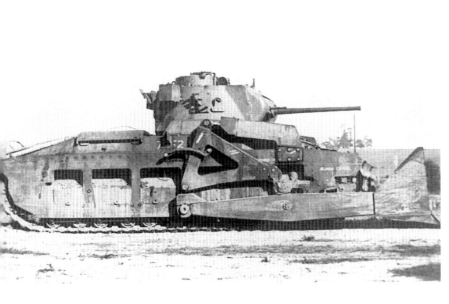

An Australian Matilda with the second type of bulldozer blade, hydraulically operated. An armoured cover is fitted over the hydraulic cylinder on each side. This is one of the relatively few Matildas to be seen in Australia with the tall cupola. (The Tank Museum, Bovington)

e special armoured turret onto a Matilda chassis, ving first removed the tank's original 2-pdr. rret. This gives some idea of the speed and ease th which this conversion could be carried out Both tanks are painted in khaki brown with ruptive areas of very dark brown. Markings on e nearest vehicle include the brown and dark een diabolo device of 35th Tank Brigade. Notice e special low-visibility monoslot headlamps ead of the original side lamps on each track ard.

Plate G: *Experimental Matilda Hedghog rocket firing tank, 4th Australian Armoured Brigade; Queensland, 1945*
The 'Projector' (Hedgehog No.1 Mark I) tank is shown with the launcher box elevated, in the process of firing a barrage of rockets at a demonstration. The Matilda is finished in the Australian dark jungle green but retains the original fording height markings and displays its British WD number in large white digits, without the initial letter T.

Matilda Frog methrower blazing away maximum range with siderable effect. Despite at was, in fact, a fairly nplicated conversion the k appears to be almost altered from the outside. he Tank Museum, vington)

INDEX

(References to illustrations are shown in **bold**. Plates are prefixed 'pl.' with commentary locators in brackets, e.g. 'pl. **C** (44-45)'.)